Havens *of* Healing

CASSIDY DIEHL

Copyright © 2018 Cassidy Diehl

Coediting by Madeline Raponi

Unless otherwise indicated, no part of this publication may be reproduced, stored in a retrieval system, or transmitted in any form or by any means, electronic, mechanical, photocopying, recording, scanning, or any information storage, without prior written permission from the Publisher.

All Rights Reserved.

ISBN-13: 978-1999474409
ISBN-10: 1999474406

*To the Star Children
on Planet Earth*

CONTENTS

Acknowledgements vii
Foreword ix
Introduction 1

Flowing Through The River
of Pain 5

Walking In The Woods of
Confusion 9

Repurposing Your Thorns of
Defensiveness 15

Stopping The Slavery of
Your Fruits 21

Escaping The Quicksand of
Sorrows 27

Forgiving Your Avalanche of
Guilt 31

Climbing The Cliff of Concern 37

Restoring Your Sun's Light 43

Mining In The Cave of
Enlightenment 47

Transforming Your Volcano
of Compression 51

Breaking Free From the
Vines of Burdens 55

Sprouting as a Weed of Unacceptance **61**

Recovering Your Moss of Wounds **67**

Reconnecting To Your Sacred Roots **73**

Clearing the Thunderstorm of Abandonment **77**

Sailing Through The Ocean of Dreams **81**

Appendix I **87**
Appendix II **91**

ACKNOWLEDGEMENT

I am forever grateful for the presence and genuine support my soul sister Angela Lopez for opening the gates to assisting the star children. You've mirrored to my soul the opportunity to lead a new generation of conscious children. You are a God sent.

To my best friend/editor Madeline Raponi, my heart is filled with so much love being in your presence and all the fun times we've spent together. Thank you for always being there for me whenever I needed your playful energy. Your heart and mine will always beat as one. You are a blessing in my life.

Thank you to my soul family Shelby Noble, Jolene Urie, Marek Chung, Leigh Taylor, Mitzy Agüero, Shyrelle Ladouceur, Austin Canfield, Kevin Garcia, Coleen Doucette. You guys are awesome!

Shout out to my sibilings Tatum, Keegan, and Max.. thank you for challenging me and the lessons you taught me, and simply for just being your crazy weird selves. Through the situations we faced together, and the times when you were going through your own journeys of growth, I claim lots of my own healing in this book from observing your actions, reactions, and perceptions. You've made my path a fascinating one.

Thank you my spiritual team and guides, my higher self, light beings, loved ones from higher dimensions, ancestors, and teacher guides, thank you thank you thank you. My life is a living wonder because of your loving support in my life.

FOREWORD

Havens of Healing is a meditative gem as it guides the reader on powerful healing journeys while exploring polar opposites. In order to know, understand and appreciate one's own experience, and therefore the possibility of another's, one must not only have experienced it ourselves, but also its opposite. One cannot feel, experience or allow Love unless one has experienced hate. Similarly, one is not likely to receive the gift, beyond the perceptual challenge, unless one moves through it, allowing for healing, integration, and embodiment of the lesson; the gem within.

In Cassidy's "Haven's of Healing," powerful healing journeys are shared that may help others navigate through polar opposites of this earth plane so they may reconnect with and flow back into... reside at their natural centre of balance. This "flowing back into" one's centre of balance is mirrored in the journeys within "Havens of Healing" such as, "Flowing through the River of Pain" to receive the gift beyond the perceptual challenge.

As an Elementary school teacher of 30 years and Energy Healer Intuitive, facilitating growth on all levels of being and witnessing perceptual challenges that children experience from within - reflected in their experiences of family and the school system educationally, emotionally, mentally, and physically... I feel the healing journeys in "Haven of Healing" may offer valuable tools and insights for children, youth and adults to explore and relate to their own personal journeys of experience to come to a deeper understanding, realization and remembrance that they have the power within themselves to transform anything by allowing and being with embracing whatever arises to flow through them without judgment, to receive the gift beyond the "quicksand to the Oasis of Serenity" that they are indeed Master Creators/alchemists of their experience. As the young people of today and their awakening consciousness is empowered with such tools, we all heal.. family members, loved ones and the next generations to come.

"May We All Live From the Sacred Heart, Through the Sacred Heart, As the Sacred Heart, Through Every Thought, Word and Deed."

Glenda-Ray Riviere
www.reikiandbeyond-glendaray.com

Introduction

This book *Havens of Healing* is a series of manuscripts of higher wisdom and visions I've translated into words to help myself with my own healing and unique challenges. These words of guidance that flowed to me have mainly been used in my life to help me heal the mental and emotional wounds of my inner child/younger self.

At first, it wasn't my intention to make this public in any way. I've written them coming from such a deep place of pain, that to show them off to the world was the last thing I thought of doing. I thought of it like reading a private diary at a conference. So, of course, I'd think that's crazy talk. Interestingly though, there came a time when a close friend of mine came to me seeking help to heal from a relationship she was in. So I decided to let her read one of my first entries. This was *Flowing Through The River of Pain* (the first chapter of this book). In my mind, I expected her to understand what I went through thinking through my ego mindset. But instead, after she read it, she tells me *"you know, what you wrote here has told me everything that I am going through and what I need to do to overcome my challenges"*. I was reading her response so confused because of my expectations. I came to the realization over time as I kept handing it to other people to read it, everyone had a unique story to tell. It was never the same interpretation, yet it was always the same meaning. For me to witness other people seeing through their own suffering beyond my own interpretation has brought a divine awareness of my own self-realization. So in a way, this has given me purpose.

When you read this book, I invite you to interpret the meaning of the entries in it however you please. The purpose of this book isn't for you to understand what I'm going through. Instead, it's to understand what you as an individual are going through.

As you read this book, if there happens to be any feelings, sensations, or memories that rise to the surface, please keep them there. Each of them works as a special guide to aid you in your healing. However the healing unfolds, is unique for each person. Nobody experiences pain or healing the same way. Yet at the same time, we all have a different interpretation of that same experience.

So in the grand scheme of it all, we aren't actually that different from each other. Not just as humans, but as nature. HoH isn't about you understanding me or anyone else. It's about you understanding yourself. You can try all you want to define what others are by what is your truth. But that doesn't mean that your truth is the same truth to them. And it's important to remember that there is no rights or wrongs in Havens of Healing. Everything and everyone is right in their own way.

Welcome to my archive.

Love, Cassidy Diehl

Flowing Through The River of Pain

When we experience pain, we cry a river of tears. It's starts off as a painful journey because when we go through the river phase, there are thousands of emotional rocks that we hit. These are river blocks that we try to overcome to allow our pain to flow through. Some of those rocks may block certain paths of our healing process as we go through the River of Pain. This is because there are still unresolved patterns you are unconsciously repeating. You are so busy trying to control where the river is supposed to go, that you keep running off track. The key is to keep a flow going. Instead of trying to control the direction of the tears of pain, just create a flow where you set them free without judging the direction they go. Let those tears guide your healing process with every emotional rock that you stumble upon.

When you run into those rocks, reflect on them. Look straight into the rock until you see yourself. When you see yourself within the rock, you will come to the realization that it isn't the rock that is stopping your flow. It is you stopping yourself. Everything in this river is a reflection of you. The moment you realize that your story lies within this River of Pain, you then have the conscious choice of how you will journey through this river. If you choose to avoid the unknown, your current will get heavier. But if you choose to just flow, your current will get lighter.

If you keep that flow going, the river will soon become less painful. You will manage to rise easily above any obstacle or emotional rock that you may encounter. Your flow won't even realize there's a block, instead it'll just be another opportunity to make a conscious choice. Choosing whether you let the emotional rock stop and pressure you, or finding a way around it. Every time you find a way around it, you collectively gather that knowledge you've learned from each rock that you pass by. Every new lesson you learned makes the next obstacle easier than the last. As you continue down that River of Pain, you become more confident in yourself because you are trusting in your healing and where your tears are flowing.

You get closer to seeing the love and the light at the end of the river in the distance. You notice that the farther you go, the lighter the path gets. That's because you are coming to the end of your River of Pain. That's when your River of Pain transforms into the Waterfall of Fortune. You weren't destined to feel all this pain because you were meant to be unlucky. All your tears that were flowing through the River of Pain, were the prerequisites for the creation of the waterfall, to become who you were destined to be. Your once felt pains have been transformed into your greatest strength. You have officially become the being you were always meant to be. Your true self.

INTENTION TO SEAL THE HEALING

My tears guide my healing
So they do
I let go to control my outcome
So I do
I flow for a softer current
So I do
My suffering has become my strength
And so it is
My blocks are healed
My river is healed
I am healed
I am, I am, I am

Walking In The Woods of Confusion

When we feel lost with ourselves, we become so desperate for the answer that we wind up in something called the Woods of Confusion. A Forest that is here to challenge your courage. A forest where you have many paths you can choose from in front of you. However, you cannot see anything further down each path except for the fog that lies within it. All these paths look the same, but they are in fact all different. Some are easier than others, and some are longer than others. The difficulty of the path you choose is depended on how well you handle the challenges that lie within them. They will challenge you more on your mental and emotional self than they will on the physical aspect. These paths are going to test your limits, until you can handle the unlimited. The opponents you are going up against is everyone. Soul against Ego. This is an opportunity to master your authenticity by embracing your differences. When you embrace your differences, it's an opportunity to leave your mark. It's an opportunity to display your uniqueness where you can express that what makes you special is that you're different from everyone else.

Just because everyone is going down the same path doesn't mean you should. Don't feel lost in the woods because your path is different from everyone else's. Enjoy feeling lost while knowing that you are heading in the right direction. If you choose to go down a path based on what others do, you will realize that all this pain and suffering are only warning signs that you are living against your own truth. Take your first step into the path you have chosen and don't let the thought of 'Lost' confuse you.

When you travel down this path, you will hit some obstacles along the way. You will trip and fall every now and then. You will need to find a way to get back on your feet repeatedly. You will hit some branches and be blocked by dead-ends on the way, so you will have to constantly come up with new solutions around those blocks. But if you continue to keep finding a way around those things, they will serve you down the road because those will be the things that help you grow. The path may look foggy. The path may look like it leads nowhere. It may feel like you are behind everyone and everything. It may feel like this is the end for you and you will never make it out of this foggy forest. But know that it is only within that path that your destiny will be revealed. Because those that follow the path with the most challenging obstacles becomes the most victorious.

As you carry on throughout the woods of confusion, doubt will occasionally sneak upon you. Doubt doesn't show up on your path to make you feel bad about yourself. Instead, it is there to challenge you to learn how to trust. Trust that even though your path may have taken the longest to overcome, none of that will matter. Because in the end, what will matter is the person that you have become from mastering those obstacles. That is what will make you triumphant after you walk out of the Woods of Confusion.

INTENTION TO SEAL THE HEALING

I take the path that's right for me

So I do

I trust where the woods are taking me

So I do

I reach greatness through my differences

So I do

My Woods is my path to triumph

And so it is

My path is safe

My outcome is safe

I am safe

I am, I am, I am

Repurposing Your Thorns of Defensiveness

As a plant, we react with Thorns of Defensiveness when we are approached by others in ways that we are afraid to face. The way we use these defensive thorns reveals to us how far we have come in our healing, showing the aftermath of when we first experienced the trauma, and how it has carried on throughout our life. We want other plants to be friends with us. But when they approach us, we shield ourselves with our thorns out of fear that they might hurt us. By pulling out the thorns before you give anyone a chance, you automatically send a message of judgement to them.

You assume what they are going to do or say without truly knowing whether their intentions are good or bad. The thorns should only be triggered in emergency cases. But instead, you are hurting others that love you out of fear that they will hurt you. This drives them away from you, yet you wonder why nobody understands you. It's because you won't let them. You've forgotten the fact that every plant is different, and every plant grows and thinks differently. Your one traumatizing plant interaction was only one seed that hurt you. So remove the perception that every plant grows the same and thinks the same.

You can't invite more love and support in your life when all you're doing is defending yourself from what scares you. So instead of using your Thorns of Defensiveness against everyone that approaches you, give everyone a chance to offer you something. If you know in your gut that their intentions are bad, and they are hurting you, then you can shield yourself with your thorns. But for now, look back when you first pulled out your thorns of defensiveness and take this moment to understand the motivation behind this defensive reaction. You can see this defense-mechanism was created by a form of fear which has traumatized you based on your first painful experience. You've carried out the trauma from this experience and have implemented the fear into all your encounters with others that have come to you. These thorns have been wrongly used ever since.

Next time when a plant approaches you, temporarily remove the trigger button for your Thorns of Defensiveness and invite them into your space with an open mind. Allow them to say what they have to say. Allow them to do what they need to do to assist you on your path. You don't necessarily need to push your thorns out or take what they offer. Just let them do what they feel they need to do. Even if what they offer is entirely irrelevant to you. Because every plant that approaches you is an opportunity to learn something new, or to help you expand your horizons and grow.

Once you make approaching more inviting, just watch as the patch of dirt you rest in alone grows into a garden of diversity, acceptance, and togetherness. This garden you've created all started the moment you healed your Thorns of Defensiveness. Instead of using them to defend yourself, you now use them to protect the plants within the garden of beings you love.

INTENTION TO SEAL THE HEALING

I allow myself to understand others views
So I do
I invite and accept others into my space
So I do
I grant my insecurities to help me grow
So I do
My thorns are built to protect not defend
And so it is
My energy is protected
My space is protected
I am protected
I am, I am, I am

Stopping The Slavery of Your Fruits

As a fruit tree, we get an intuitive urge to nourish as many individuals as we can. We already know how valuable our heart of giving is when it comes to helping others that need help. You feel it is your destiny to nurture and feed those everywhere around you. But when you begin to take on so many duties, it becomes unbearable to manage. Once you give away your fruit to everyone, you don't stop there. You then start giving away your leaves, and then giving up your branches and you don't realize you have allowed other's helplessness to become your problem. This pattern is no longer serving.

This pattern has become a form of slavery. As soon as you begin to lose control, that's when your experience burn-out. This challenge is about finding the balance between giving and self-care.

To avoid that burn-out, set yourself some boundaries on how many fruits you will give away. Set boundaries for when you need to temporarily stop serving to recharge your branches and fruit. When you set boundaries for yourself, others will respect you. Nobody expects you to be a continually super-charged tree that never runs out of energy, and yet, you have set an expectation on yourself much higher than you can handle. It doesn't mean you're weak, or that you can't be helpful, of course it's good that you want to help as many individuals as you can. But when you position yourself to fix everyone around you, you help nobody.

You may have forgotten, you are not the only type of fruit tree in the world. In fact, there are many different fruit trees out there. As a fruit tree, you can help with many things. But you can't expect yourself to be a multi-fruit tree when you were born with the gift of growing one species of fruit. You can try to be more than one fruit tree, but you'll never really see the power that's within you already. Be open to sending others in another direction. Even if you annoy others and you can't meet their needs. It's better to send others in another direction while you recharge in the meantime. Look at it this way. If you tried serve them while you had nothing to give, they would be greatly disappointed. That's a result which you and everyone else would much rather avoid. Remember this. When you don't own your power, you give permission for others to take advantage of you. But when you do own your power, you give permission for others to appreciate you.

So stop the slavery. Start owning the gifts that you were born with. Instead of making yourself available for everyone's needs, reconnect with your body. Give yourself time to recharge when there's not enough fruit to feed those around you. Develop a system where you will never have to worry about disappointing everyone. By doing this, you become more effective in your serving. Serve those who need your fruit. Don't give to anyone who needs a different fruit than your own. If all the giving gets overwhelming, all you need to do is tell them that, for now, you have nothing left to offer them, and you need to recharge. You don't need to help everyone at the same time. They won't be annoyed or disappointed because they can see that you are only one tree. You can only give so much at a time. You see, slavery is others controlling us to give on their terms. But service is when you are in control of yourself and give on your own terms. You're not meant to be a Fruit Tree of Slavery. You are a Fruit Tree of Service.

INTENTION TO SEAL THE HEALING

I own the gifts I was born with
So I do
I allow myself to recharge
So I do
I set myself energetic boundaries
So I do
I control the fruits I give away
So I do
My Fruits are my gift of service
And so it is
My fruits are replenished
My energy is replenished
I am replenished
I am, I am, I am

Escaping The Quicksand of Sorrows

┼◯┼┼

When our suffering overpowers our mind, we wind up in something called the Quicksand of Sorrows. It's a trap that we unintentionally fall into when we get lost within our suffering. The quicksand of sorrows is formed by three things. The Clay which creates your pain, the Water which forms your reactions, and the Sand which controls your mind. You need to understand the mindset in which these three things manifest, and what is causing you to suffer before you can escape the quicksand.

The Clay is the beginning of all the suffering. When the Clay of Pain shows up in our path, it is really here to help us overcome outside influences. The Water of Reactions is there to help us process, how we choose to respond to the Clay of Pain. If you knew yourself well enough, the clay would have been dissolved. But instead, you chose to react by believing what the Clay of Pain told you. Because of this now you've trapped yourself in the Sand of Thought. Our mind will believe whatever you tell it, and will form new thoughts based on how you've reacted. When you get into the sand of thought, your mind merges the pain, the reactions, and the beliefs about yourself all into a sinkhole of quicksand and sorrows. Remember that every burden you decide to carry in your mind gives more power to the quicksand That, as a result makes you closer to burying yourself alive in your sorrows and suffering.

Escaping the quicksand of sorrows is a process of staying calm during agitation and letting go of what is weighing us down. You can't fix a problem with the same mindset that created it. Therefore, to move forward you need to change the way you approach escaping the quicksand. As you continue to calm yourself down from your agitation, your sorrows will begin to reveal themselves more clearly. You will be able to see where they came from, what is causing them to stick to you, and what you need to do to let them go. Review these sorrows carefully, because how you choose to face them is entirely up to you. Know that if you react by pushing them deeper in the quicksand, they will grab onto you and make you sink with them. Whereas if you let them rise to the surface with the patience to see what they can teach you, you can set them free and release the heaviness that's making you sink.

So now is the time to surrender the suffering. With every burden you invite with understanding, you can decide how you want the pain to pass by you. Every time you release a burden, you begin to float higher. You can feel the weight of all this quicksand letting you go, as you release your agitation. The quicksand only wants to suck up those that suffer in sorrows. But now that you've chosen to not to take those sorrows personally and ruin your inner peace, you can finally swim yourself out.

Now that you've escaped the Quicksand, watch the sorrows in the quicksand dissipate and die. Notice how now as you watch them sink, it no longer affects your sense of being. Those sorrows were never a part of who you are internally. They were only perceptions of a false outside influence which you decided to believe were true. You are not the Quicksand of Sorrows. You are the Oasis of Serenity.

INTENTION TO SEAL THE HEALING

I choose to stay calm in agitation
So I do
I set my sorrows free and release them
So I do
Nobody controls my beliefs except for me
So I do
I chose peace over pain
So I do
I surrender the quicksand from my mind
And so it is
My sorrows are released
My thoughts are released
I am released
I am, I am, I am

Forgiving Your Avalanche of Guilt

When we do something that hurts others unintentionally, we cause an Avalanche of Guilt. This guilt carries the wrongs that we have done and backfires onto us as shame. Because we have already created this avalanche, we can't exactly take back our actions, the snow has already tumbled on top of those that we hurt. The amount of guilt you are carrying from this avalanche is devastating you. Mainly because you feel ashamed of yourself and regretful because you are responsible for this snowfall.

You are so busy digging inside the snow,

trying to fix everything about the disaster you created. No matter how much you dig, you won't recover anything but guilt, shame and regret for your actions. The fact that you feel guilty is actually healthy because it shows you that what you did was wrong. It shows you that you care, and that you want to make up for your mistakes. You reacted wrong and you've acknowledged that, which is good. But now isn't a time to fix as much as it is a time to learn. Stop dwelling in the shame and bad feelings about what you could have done but didn't. Suffering in the snowfall will only continue to make you feel worse about what you have done, without affecting any positive change.

Look at the snow of shame and review its journey. Go back to the top of the mountain where it started. The snow was up there glistening in peaceful stillness, you interfered its peace in some way, and so it fell. So use this moment to review how exactly you caused the avalanche, and why you chose this particular approach. At the root of your heart, you know the motivation behind this action. You can see how it might have been beneficial from your end. But at the time, you were unable to see how it may not have been quite the same from the others perspective. Now that the avalanche has happened, you wish you could take back your actions.

Now that you see the origin of the snow's journey, take a step back from the fallen snow. This moment is your time to make things officially right. How you choose to leave behind this avalanche is up to you. You can leave it as an Avalanche of Guilt, or an Avalanche of Lessons. You can transform your guilt right here, into forgiveness right now. Use this avalanche to learn from your mistakes. Take these actions that you took to cause this avalanche of guilt and use them to enhance your knowledge and learn from the experience. Let the situation move behind you, as that is where it needs to be. When you bring a bad experience of the past into your present, it becomes guilt. But when you leave a bad experience in your past, it stays as a learning experience. Bless the avalanche for teaching you all that it has taught you, then walk away from it. Now that you have forgiven the avalanche for falling, now you will never have to experience or carry the burden of shame, guilt and regret ever again.

INTENTION TO SEAL THE HEALING

My shame shows that I care
So I do
The snow has fallen
So I accept that
I take responsibility for my actions
So I do
My intentions remain pure at heart
So they do
My mistakes transformed into lessons
My guilt transformed into forgiveness
And so it is
My avalanche is forgiven
My actions are forgiven
I am forgiven
I am, I am, I am

Climbing The Cliff of Concern

When we fear the worst-case in the future of our dreams, we wind up on something called the Cliff of Concern. The Cliff of Concern is a climb which tests you on your fears. At the very top of the Cliff is a gift known as View of Victory. However, we cannot access the View of Victory unless we climb the Cliff of Concern and master the art of fear.

With every rock we step on as we climb the Cliff of Concern, there is the chance of either slipping or rising. Either the rock is controlling you, or you are controlling the rock. When the rock controls you, it's because your fear of slipping is overpowering you. When you focus on not wanting the rock to slip, you are unconsciously envisioning the rock slipping. Therefore, your intention is for it to slip and so, it does. Before you take a step onto the rock, set your intention on how you want that rock to respond to you. Make the rock become your servant as if you are its Great Master. It must do exactly as you tell it. Set the intention that you want it to be stable where it is and imagine it giving you that extra boost. You will see that by setting your attention on what you want to happen, you get what you want. Keep climbing and master every rock as you make your way.

You may notice that the higher you climb, the steeper the surface is. You will come across some Rocky Ledges that will try and scare you into looking down. They aren't here to ruin your climb. Instead they are here to help you master Comfort Zone Destruction. They want to see you overcome an obstacle where you are risking for the reward you know. They will keep challenging you until they think you are ready for the gift you've been dreaming of. You may find yourself wanting to take the safest route on the Cliff of Concern because you want to face the least amount of challenges. Even though you might think that you're getting closer by taking the route that comforts you the most, it is slowing you down more than it is speeding you up. If you want to grow, you need to be uncomfortable. When the Rocky Ledges see you not making much progress, that will be the moment when they appear. So when they appear before you, take on their challenge. It may be tougher to climb, but it will be faster as well as helping you grow. Continue mastering every rock you step on and every cliff you climb, knowing that all these obstacles are making you stronger and making you fearless for what is to come.

You will notice as you look beyond the horizon, you are now above the clouds. This is a sign that you've risen above your fears finally. You realize that there is only one last platform for you to reach. This platform is the View of Victory. Swing from the cliff-hangers, climb the rocks and land. Now before you celebrate, just sit there for a minute a look down below you. You can see every rock that you stepped on, and you can see every rocky ledge you climbed. You can also see every possible route that you could have taken to get here. Comparing from all the path's you could have taken and the path that you chose to take, you may have thought in the moment is was the wrong way all along. But instead, it was the path you were supposed to climb. The unique challenges you faced within them were there to make you strong in your mind and your heart. You have officially conquered your fights, your fears, and your fuss. You can now surrender all the concern that may arise down your life path into faith. Knowing that you will become who you are meant to be.

INTENTION TO SEAL THE HEALING

Every rock helps me ascend
So they do
Every ledge makes me fearless
So they do
My challenges are conquered
So they are
My frights are conquered
So they are
My fears have transformed into faith
And so it has
My steps are victorious
My climb is victorious
I am victorious
I am, I am, I am

Restoring Your
Suns Light

┼◉┼

As the Sun, it's within your heart to be a source of light that shines upon others. When we see beings who need an extra light, we are always there for them. That's your whole purpose. But by giving so much light, we often become so giving that others begin to take advantage of us. To the extent that they start to use you for their own greed. They become so unappreciative of your light that they steal all of you, until you are dimmed to darkness. When it comes to that point, that it doesn't matter how much sunlight you provide for someone. When they use you for greed and selfishness, you are no longer a gift of rejuvenation. Instead you are a tool used for ego. You feel so drained that you become afraid to shine your light on others out of fear that they will treat you the same. Don't let the darkness of a being who resents you dim your light. Remember, you are the Sun. You need to own your light with pride. Just because they are destructive doesn't mean you should use your heat to burn those ungrateful beings alive. Because remember, if you don't provide light to one being, you don't provide light to anybody. Without you, the world would suffer significantly. When you use anger as a response, everyone around you becomes affected. Your purpose is to shine your light and love. So be there for them. Even though there are beings out there who use your light for stroking their ego, just shine anyway.

When you need to, use the time in darkness to restore your sun's light and love. So when the next day comes around, you will rise stronger than you were yesterday. Use that following morning as an opportunity to set a new intention, to be a source for those who appreciate you lighting up their life. Anybody else who will end up using your light for selfishness and greed will get nothing but reflected shadows of their own darkness. They won't see their shadows right away, but other beings around them will. Their darkness will mirror back to them in ways that will shock them. The crowd will begin to see beyond the ego, where you as the sun will become the spotlight.

In the end, when it's time for you to restore your sun's light and the sky gets dark, those who live in ego will be lost looking down into darkness. But those who live in soul will be guided by your light when they look up at the moon. It becomes a reminder for them that even though you're not physically seen during the night, your presence will be felt and your reflection off the moon will protect them throughout their dreams. So when the morning comes around once you are restored, you wake them up and say "I'm here to light up your day". Then you get to watch the all the smiles, laughter, and healing you bring to the world. That is the greatest gift you can provide as the Sun. There is always a being that loves you for what you provide.

INTENTION TO SEAL THE HEALING

I am appreciated for what I provide

So I am

I shine beyond the darkness

So I do

My response is always love

So it is

My Light is a gift of rejuvenation

And so it is

My service is Light

My energy is Light

I am Light

I am, I am, I am

Mining In The Cave of Enlightenment

When we lose our sense of self, we search to find ourselves in a place called the Cave of Enlightenment. This cave is here to teach us the path to finding the answers within ourselves. Before you enter the cave, you feel the need to prepare yourself for what lies ahead by bringing all your tools to dig and drill. You enter the cave and you start mining. You dig and find nothing but dirt. You drill and find nothing but coal. You continue digging and drilling in desperation to find something that you can claim as worthiness. But all that you find is emptiness. You notice after a while that the more you mine, the less you find. You can't expect yourself to achieve enlightenment when all what you're doing is digging holes inside of yourself. You are just destroying yourself even more. Sure, you may find some coal here and there. But forcing yourself to dig holes just for the sake of finding something, will never give you what you seek. As soon as you discipline yourself out of the expectation of finding something right now, you can go about journeying through the cave of enlightenment a bit differently. Drop the tools and surrender yourself deep in the darkness in this cave. Walk through carefully because you are going to enter the darkest part of your path. You may hear rocks fall down from the ceiling, you may slip into some cave leakages, and feel the fragility of the pillars you hang onto. But all these things that come before you in this darkness show up as pieces of the journey of enlightenment. So just keep going.

As you go through the darkness of the mine, you are going to have to start becoming reliant on solely on your intuition and self-awareness. Because you're unable to physically see what lies ahead, you need to use your senses to be one with the darkness of the cave. So embrace the progress you are making, and the path you are walking inside this cave. You will start to notice the patterns and behaviors of the cave. You will gain a sense of knowing when those leaks and breakdowns will occur, how they occur, and what aspects of yourself causes them. You can now use this knowledge to progress even further into the Cave of Enlightenment.

As you walk deeper through the cave, your awareness begins tuning into the end of the cave of enlightenment. After all the suffering the cave has put you through, the cave then reveals its soul to you. You begin to feel lighter, and you see a massive glowing crystal with your soul signature on it. You realize that this cave was demonstrating to you everything that you are. It taught you that. Unlike in the beginning, when you were so desperate to find something material to claim as your worthiness. You learned that to find yourself, you had to give up the tools of destruction you were carrying, and bravely tune into your darkness. Which in the end, showed you beyond the depths of suffering. There always lies a treasure of enlightenment buried within you.

INTENTION TO SEAL THE HEALING

I give up the tools of self-destruction
So I do
I surrender all forms of expectation
So I do
My self-awareness brings me self-knowing
So it does
The answers I seek are all within me
And so it is
My darkness is at peace
My cave is at peace
I am at peace
I am, I am, I am

Transforming Your Volcano of Compression

When we feel hesitant to express ourselves, we are backed by the fear of others judging us, so we become a Volcano of Compression. We have this desire to be accepted and liked by everyone. But because that is impossible, we get caught in this losing game that holds us back from experiencing and expressing our true selves. By compressing your magma, you nourish your fear by hiding who you are to avoid embarrassment. Sure, by hiding your magma, you will never have to worry about being embarrassed. But that also means you will never get to experience authentic expression of your true self. Nobody will ever know the greatness within your core.

There will always be judgement outside of ourselves. But whether you choose to accept those judgements will affect where you stand as a Volcano of Compression. It may seem like letting your magma erupt is the hardest thing to do. You're continuously surrounded by critics who disgrace the thought of you erupting because of the mess you will make. However, the longer you hold onto your magma, the less confident you will feel about yourself. Yes, you are a volcano that compresses its magma for a short while. But that's not what you are meant to do your whole life. Eventually, your magma will have to erupt onto the surface. You are a volcano, and you can only compress so much magma before you'll explode. You already know what you need to do to express yourself, yet you are hesitant to erupt.

Release yourself from focusing on the worst-case scenario. The future outcome hasn't happened yet, so release your mind from the assumptions of what awful things could happen. All these fears of judgement and opinions are only making you undervalue yourself.

If you live up to other's expectations of who they think you should be, you will only be able to express yourself as much as they allow you to. So for now, shift your focus away from their opinions. Surrender the thoughts of who others think you're supposed to be and allow your magma to flow out. As you strip your ego bare, all that's left is your essence of Love.

Now is your moment to erupt. Show the world the beauty of your lava. Notice how flooding your magma outside of your core was the hardest, yet easiest and most freeing thing you have ever done. This is what it means to be a volcano. Others outside may not enjoy the process of your eruption. But that won't matter to you because every eruption you go through is a rebirth into becoming more you. You have officially transformed from a Volcanic Compression of Judgement into a Volcanic Eruption of Freedom. This is the truest essence of who you are as a Volcano.

INTENTION TO SEAL THE HEALING

The need of acceptance is surrendered
So it is
The opinions of me are surrendered
So they are
The hesitation to erupt is surrendered
So it is
Erupting frees me to express my true self
And so it does
My Lava is expressive
My Magma is expressive
I am expressive
I am, I am, I am

Breaking Free From The Vines of Burdens

╂◉╂

When we carry the emotional burdens of others, we get knotted in the Vines of Burdens. These vines were never meant to be worn around you, but what has happened was you got so involved in their struggle, that the vines began stretching their way to you. The vines are now stuck on you because you attracted the burden of your other influences onto you. It's in your greatest interest to help others with the emotional trouble they are going though. But as soon as you take on these responsibilities as if their problems are yours, it can be extremely difficult to unwrap ourselves from these vines. It's not your duty to fix their situation. You know this burden was never meant to be yours to carry. Yet in a way, you feel like you are the only one who can properly solve this burden. Because of this, you vibrationally trick the Vines of Burden to wrap themselves around you. And so they do.

To properly untangle these vines, there's two parts you need to develop. The first is your Emotional Trimmers. This is meant to cut the emotional cords of the vines. It may seem difficult to cut them because by cutting these vines, you also cut your emotions. These trimmers aren't meant to make you emotionless, but instead it's to tell the vines that by cutting these burdens off you, they are no longer needed. You are essentially telling them that these emotional burdens are not meant to be yours, and you need them to stop tangling you. The vines then begin to untangle themselves from you. Feel the burden within you, and come face to face with these feelings. Remember how peaceful your life was before these vines came into play? This peacefulness is still and has always been there. This is where you make your choice to escape living their life of burdens. You have a life of your own you need to take responsibility for. This is when you take out the trimmers and cut the vines. Not because you don't care about them, but because you need to take care of yourself first.

Now you need to build your Emotional Fence. This is a fence that makes the Vines of Burdens impossible grow over. Since you recently cut the vines, now you need to make sure that the Vines of Burdens never chase after you again in the future. This shield-mechanism will protect you from any emotional burdens that surround you. So even if you begin to feel you need to carry responsibility, you will know how to make yourself a barrier the vines can't pass. Because you are no longer tangled up, gather all the supplies you need to construct your fence. Build this unbreakable impassable fence around your emotional body and keep it there.

Now for the next time you catch yourself near the Vines of Burdens, feel the emotional burden with understanding within the vines. You can clearly see the suffering of the individual. So instead of taking on their burdens as your own, wish the situation well, and things will resolve organically.

Accept the fact that it isn't your problem to solve or to worry about. This is what positive detachment is all about. You have officially been freed from the Vines of Burdens.

INTENTION TO SEAL THE HEALING

The vines I cut are released
So they are
The vines I fence up are blocked
So they are
I let go of responsibilities that aren't mine
So I do
Positive detachment frees me
And so it does
The burdens are freed
The vines are freed
I am freed
I am, I am, I am

Sprouting As A Weed of Unaccpetance

Like any other plant, we have phases of growth. When others abuse us during our growth, they label us as a weed. They call you a weed because they only see a part of you. This is the phase where you are preparing to amaze everyone. Unfortunately, this phase takes the longest. So what happens is they get impatient and forcefully remove you from the garden. They remove you because they think all you do is cause trouble for the rest of the garden. Every time you want to shine your light, others make it nearly impossible to see your value. It doesn't matter how many times you get dug up, you never seem to find the place where you can blossom to your full potential. Of all the gardens you've tried growing in, nobody gives you the chance to fully sprout. Eventually, you will find a garden that accepts you.

Instead of moving to the 'already-grown' gardens, move to an environment where there's nothing but dirt. Move to this empty plot of dirt because here, nothing has been touched, nothing has flourished, and because nothing has been taken out. You may feel hesitant to go anywhere at this point because you don't want to be shut down and hurt again. But just trust that you can still grow even when nobody is there for you.

Choose your spot on this land and grow as you always have. Notice how much farther you have gotten in your growth, compared to all the other environments you previously tried to grow in? The only difference with this environment is that there is nothing here to judge you or dig you up. It's just you. These phases of growth may be tougher because you are alone in these conditions, but the advantage to this is that you can spend as much time as you need to go through these phases of growth. You are no longer living on anybody else's timeline except your own. Your timeline is the only one you should live by.

The more you grow, the more you begin to see potential in the plant you are becoming. A colourful bud begins to blossom. Your need for external validation is no longer a part of you because you are blooming into the plant you were meant to be. A Flower of Abundance. Now that you have finally bloomed, everyone who passes by you appreciates your presence. This is what the gift of acceptance feels like. Those who have called you a weed now see you at your fullest, now feel a deep guilt. They regret the abuse they caused by digging you out, now that they can see your happiness and their emptiness. They secretly wish you were there. But now you have no need to go back there, because you are the new spotlight and not them.

You have learned from this journey of unacceptance that these past flowers all had a home that was chosen for them. But that didn't mean you belonged there too. All you had to do was go somewhere that chose you, so you could grow to reach your full potential.

A place that you could call home. You weren't meant to be a weed in someone else's garden. You were meant to be the spotlight flower of an expansive land of dirt, to be the garden that land was meant to become.

INTENTION TO SEAL THE HEALING

I can grow even when I'm alone
So I can
I only focus on my timeline of growth
So I do
I have bloomed and reached my potential
So I have
My phase as a weed has passed
Because now I am a flower
And so it is
My garden is accepted
My land is accepted
I am accepted
I am, I am, I am

Recovering Your Moss of Wounds

When times of suffering and brokenness happen to us, our Moss of Wounds is formed. Our moss grows on us when there's an area of our life that hasn't had very much light shining upon it. The darkness there transforms into moss and stays there as a mark of experience. We often don't like the way it works. So, what happens is we view our moss as a bad thing and we keep it covered up. However, by covering up your wounds, you become more insecure and can only look at these wounds of moss as a weakness.

When you speak upon your moss as a weakness, that is the image you subconsciously tell others to see. Your insecurity of owning your marks of moss speaks a lot about how you perceive yourself and your challenges. It's a meaning that you made up and believed. Because you believed your moss was unworthy, it materialized in that negative way. So now that's how everyone else sees it.

There is no need for you to have standards of flawlessness. Nobody expects perfection out of you, so you shouldn't expect it either. Ultimately, everything in nature has a flaw of its own. But the only difference is that every other being in nature doesn't use their flaws against themselves to make them less valuable. Every being comes up with a way they can use that flaw to their own advantage. They place a different meaning to their wounds that brings out the gifts within them. Remember, you don't get wounds to make you weak. You get wounds to make you wise.

To properly heal the moss, you need to change the meaning of this moss so you can feel empowered by it. Instead of telling the world the story of how your moss of wounds have made you weak, tell the story of how you have transformed your biggest weakness into your greatest strength. Because you've already constructed the sad beginning of your story, now you need to construct and live the happy ending. Typically when there's something that's blocking you from healing, there's an opportunity to create a new beginning. Your moss can't properly heal itself as a wound unless put into the light where the positive meaning is.

So take off the mask and let your moss be seen. Show the light your Moss with your new empowering story to diminish the darkness within it. Let the light bathe your moss as it cleanses the wounds. See how much of a difference it makes when you change the meaning of your moss. Before you perceived your moss as a reason you weren't worthy. But now it is the reason you are worthy. It is the reason you are stronger than you were in the past. You can see now that without this moss, you wouldn't have become the being you are today. You would be weaker without the moss.

For all the moss marks that you receive in the future, you now know how to transform any moss into something more meaningful.

So the next time someone calls out your moss as a wound, you can tell them, wrong. It is now the Moss of Wisdom.

INTENTION TO SEAL THE HEALING

I give my wounds a positive meaning
So I do
I keep my mask removed
So I do
My moss of experience is why I am worthy
So I am
My wounds became my wisdom
And so it is
My wounds are recovered
My moss is recovered
I am recovered
I am, I am, I am

Reconnecting To Your Sacred Roots

Just like a tree, when we first seed into this world with love and beauty in our heart, all of us look the same. As we start to send shoots above the soil, we then begin to look around outside of ourselves and realize how abstract and separated we are as individual trees. We take on judgments based on the physical appearances of our fellow trees and we label them and ourselves as if we don't belong. There will be times when other trees will call you out as being too this or too that. You will feel so pressured by the labels other trees put on you that you start believing them. All you want deep in your roots is to feel a sense of belonging. Don't fall into the trap of wanting to fit in. You weren't born to fit in. Instead of using the harassment that you receive as a motivation to rise above them, you let the crowd tower over you and blind you. You've forgotten where your roots are connected.

Now, use this time to reconnect with your sacred roots. Replay your journey from before these breeds of other trees influenced you negatively. Remember as a seed, you didn't think about what your fellow peers were doing and what were thinking. You stayed one with your roots, you were grounded, you knew who you were, and you knew what you were already worth. But as soon as the other trees showed up and started the harassment, you unconsciously gave them permission to do so. So now is your chance to change your story based on how you choose to face the destruction. You are not the outer self, separated from everything, that part which only they can see. You are the inner self with roots united with everything, that which only you can see.

So yes, let them harass you, block your light, and stand in your way. Don't respond to the peer pressure. Stay connected to your roots and stand with pride, whatever they throw at you. By standing tall while they break your branches, and taking pride in who you are, you show your own strength. It demonstrates that whatever happens outside of yourself, your inner power and self knowledge remains strong. All this outer destruction will only become a reflection of their own weakness, lack of groundedness, disconnection from themselves, and of how deep an illusion they are living.

When you accept and respect your flaws, you oversee the flaws of other trees and you accept and respect them as well. Because the thing you have awakened and realized is that all the roots of every tree are connected and planted within the same surface. By reconnecting to your sacred roots, you become an expansion of unity and bring us all together.

INTENTION TO SEAL THE HEALING

I take pride in who I am

So I do

I remain connected to my roots within me

So I do

I stay aligned with my roots

Strong with my roots

One with my roots

And so it is

My roots are grounded

My self-worth is grounded

I am grounded

I am, I am, I am

Clearing The Thunderstorm of Abandonment

╫◉╟

When our loyalty to something turns against us as a cloud of carelessness, we become trapped in a situation called the Thunderstorm of Abandonment. This storm is created inside of us when those that we care about most unexpectedly stop caring for us. Your caring temperature is warm-hearted. Once you feel the cold-hearted temperature within those that you loved deeply, they shock you in bursts of lightning. You may have thought both of your hearts were a part of the same cloud. Only to be blindsided by being completely opposite clouds. The amount of abandonment you feel within, you can't help but cry raindrops, and scream thunder. It all happened so suddenly. You've been struck by the force of abandonment.

You are now faced with a whole new challenge that lies ahead of you. This thunderstorm you're in right now is testing you on your strength during detachment. Look at yourself from the ground up and watch the way you're responding to these tragic events. The thunder you scream is your anger. The lightning that strikes you are external influences that affect you. The raindrops that you shed are your sadness. Analyze yourself in each piece of this storm.

Remember, this thunderstorm you have temporarily become was originally caused by your warm-hearted temperature mixing with the cold-hearted ones. So the only reason you are still a living thunderstorm is because you are still holding onto the abandonment and loneliness influenced by the cold-hearted peers you warm-heartedly loved. You are spending all your time and energy being there for others. Others that don't bother to put that same energy into being there for you. Invite the wind into the storm so you can blow them away. Instead of looking at them as a loss, look at this emotional experience as a form of positive detachment. Release your need to be with them. Let them go. Not because you don't care, but because they don't. Having the cold-hearted careless in your cloud is a waste of energy. With every form of coldness that you release, your thunderstorm starts to get calmer. Your heart starts to get warmer. As your heart warms up, the sun begins to breakthrough. That's where your darkest times become celebrated.

What makes others excited to watch you suffer a thunderstorm of abandonment isn't about the suffering, it's about the journey you took to transform from a rainstorm into a rainbow. A journey from loneliness to supportiveness. They're inspired to watch you because they know that eventually, no matter how long it takes, you will shine once again after battling your darkness. And so will they.

INTENTION TO SEAL THE HEALING

I blow away all that no longer serves me
So I do
I release coldness from my heart
So I do
I receive warmth in my heart
So I do
My thunder of anger is released
My rain of saddness is released
The abandonment I felt is released
And so it is
My battles are cleared
My storm is cleared
I am cleared
I am, I am, I am

Sailing Through The Ocean of Dreams

The Ocean of Dreams is merely a journey that we take to reach our dreams. Every beach connected to this ocean is someone's dream ready to be fulfilled. But unfortunately, not everyone has completed the journey. Only do the most courageous of them all make it out alive, arriving at their beach with their dreams fulfilled.

The ocean current starts off calm and easy in the beginning. You feel the presence of relaxation and tranquility as you set out. But as you sail farther, you run into the hefty Tidal Waves of Discouragement. They are called that because they give you reasons and excuses not to follow your dream. These tidal waves come crashing into you, because they want you to go back to where they think you belong. They're afraid of you taking risky chances, so they push you in the opposite direction, back to shore where it's safe. In your heart, you want all the waves in the ocean to be a part of helping you reach your dream. But that doesn't mean they will.

During the time you spend in the Ocean of Dreams, you don't choose what waves come across you. Instead, they choose you. Sometimes the waves of discouragement will choose you because they see you as an easy target to send back to shore, or they see your commitment as too intimidating. They think you're crazy. They're afraid to watch you succeed because it reflects to them that even as a tidal wave, they themselves have never been able to reach their dreams. They're afraid to witness someone close to them act courageously on something meaningful for themselves, which they haven't ever had the courage to face. The act of you achieving your dreams scares something insecure deep inside those who discourage you.

It's not your duty to stay on their level of fear. It's your duty to rise above every tidal wave of discouragement that approaches you. Instead of drowning in the waves as they tower over you, hold your breath with faith and float above them. The Ocean of Dreams can be difficult to navigate with all these tidal waves. But to make sure you're on the right track, find a way to sail past them. Ride the tide and let the waves guide you to your destination. Use their appearances as a signal that you are a wave closer to your dream. The direction you see them coming from, is the direction you need to go. Because where these waves discourage you from going, is exactly where you are supposed to go. You may feel tempted to go back. But you didn't come this far, only to turn around. Keep overcoming every tidal wave that discourages you. As you master each wave, you feel it gets easier and easier.

But now comes the big one; The Tsunami of Failure. This wave has been titled this because it's the checkpoint that makes most of those sailing through the Ocean of Dreams head back to shore where it's safe. The Tsunami of Failure has conquered everyone who has had the guts to face it. Therefore, their end-result becomes failure. This is the wave which all your past Tidal Waves of Discouragement have been trying to make you avoid. Just beyond this tsunami wave is the beach that has been calling you this whole time.

Look at this Tsunami. Its getting closer every breath you take. This is the line that determines the fate of your dreams. Success or Failure. Approach it now. Instead of focusing on the tsunami being in the way, focus on reaching your dream. The tsunami may be physically bigger than you, but your dreams are massively bigger than the tsunami. That's what will make you rise above the Tsunami of Failure. Use all your might on the success of your dreams and set sail.

Then comes forth the Tsunami of Failure. In the Tsunami you go. In the Tsunami you face. Out the tsunami you challenge. Out the tsunami you break free.

You have officially conquered the Tsunami of Failure. Welcome to the beach of your dreams.

INTENTION TO SEAL THE HEALING

I let the waves guide me to my destination

So I do

I ascend every wave that discourages me

So I do

The waves are defeated

The Tsunami is defeated

And so it is

My journey is fulfilled

My dreams are fulfilled

I am fulfilled

I am, I am, I am

APPENDIX I

Havens of Healing Exercises:

I strive to bring Havens of Healing in as many places and forms as I can. I warmly invite you to bring these exercises into your life, where ever Havens of Healing suits you. Some of these areas can be your business, career, relationships, the classroom, non-profits, clubs/groups, hospitals, etc..

PS: Share your *Havens of Healing* on social media with **#HavensOfHealing**

Group - Healing Circle

a) *Have one person in the group read any one of the chapters, while everyone else in the group closes their eyes and listens.* **(play meditation music quietly in the back ground to relax everyone's mind for more clarity)**

b) *After the person reads the story, take turns describing your own Haven of Healing based on what you have experienced during this reading, what you learned about yourself, and what you realize you need to do to over come your challenges.*

Group/Solo - Crisis Cleansing

a) *When in an argumental crisis with another person, take an hour or two alone and find a chapter in Havens of Healing describing the situation you as an individual are feeling/experiencing.*

b) *When you have both found a chapter that resonates with understanding your individual perceptions, both of you take turns expressing your Haven of Healing on why you reacted the way you did, said the things you said, and did the things you did.*

Solo - Revealing the Healing

a) *When you are experiencing any kind of suffering (whether it is physical, mental, emotional or spiritual), yet you're unable to figure out where you need healing or what is causing you to feel such way. Hold the book in your hands.*

b) *Set an intention to the book to reveal where you need to heal. (Perform this intention however you like.)*

c) *When you feel ready, close your eyes. Performing without judgement, flip to a random page and put your finger anywhere on the page.*

d) Now open your eyes. The page you opened, will have the healing you need. It will either be the sentence your finger landed on, the paragraph, or the whole thing. Your intuition will tell you the sign.

<u>Solo - 16-Day HoH Challenge</u>

For 16 consecutive days, read a chapter of this book a day, and express your personal Haven of Healing in whatever way you like. So after 16 days, you have recorded a collective series of your healing.

Ex #1: *Write a page per chapter. After 16 days, combine them in an essay, journal or story of your healing.*

Ex #2: *Draw a picture per chapter. After 16 days, combine them in an artbook of your healing.*

Ex #3: *Take a photo per chapter. After 16 days, combine them into a photo album or collage of your healing.*

OPTIONAL: To feature your story on my *Havens of Healing Community* Pinterest Board, submit a photo or video of your HOH Challenge to the following:
hohsubmissions@gmail.com

Extra - Havens of Healing: Unified Perceptions Gallery

The HoH Unified Perceptions Gallery is an online gallery sharing Havens of Healing reader's their own individual healing experiences and stories, which are categorized for different Haven's of Healing Chapters. To add your Haven of Healing to Gallery, follow the instructions on the following link:
CassidyDiehl.com/hoh-gallery-submission

APPENDIX II

On Going Work With Cassidy

I want to share the numerous avenues available for you to recieve this material so you can experience the power of the latest knowledge I'm working with.

Lightwork Media

Lightwork Media is Cassidy's intensive media production branch that works on projects, businesses, campaigns and non-profit organizations which gears towards re-constructing the Golden Age. Cassidy does collaborative work mainly with lightworkers and spiritual visionaries. If you've got a soul-wrenching idea that will consciously awaken humanity and help unify the world, send Cassidy a proposal at her website: *www.LightworkMedia.com*

Private Sessions

In private sessions with me, I serve in a place I call 'Center' which is my non-physical portal I consciously work in, between the physical and cosmic realms. In Center, I am in touch with both my physical self and my celestial self, so I can cope to solve the puzzles and challenges you face in the physical world from a cosmic point of view. These sessions unfold differently for each individual soul.

Every time I teach, something new comes through me. I'm able to share my latest insights and experiences in each session. You can book a session with me at:
CassidyDiehl.com/private-sessions

Event Bookings

Cassidy is available for school visits, keynote speeches and hosting tailored workshops. These events can be focused on working with Havens of Healing, or any spiritual topics you'd like Cassidy to speak about. You can inquire booking Cassidy for your event or place of business at the following link:
CassidyDiehl.com/bookings

Children of Consciousness Show

Do you have a spiritually-gifted child, but not sure how to cope with their highly advanced spiritual intelligence? Now is your chance to learn about these star kids on a mental, emotional, and spiritual level. From the universal knowledge they hold, to working with them in the physical world. Listen to Cassidy and her partner Angela in this conscious-expanding podcast as they teach the importance of the gifts these special kids hold to serve and unite the galaxy. Listen to their episodes @ soundcloud.com/childrenofconsciousness

E-Newsletter

I send out a newsletter each month giving a brief synopsis of what I am doing, events I'm hosting or attending, and new content I release to help you take your next steps on your journey of ascension.

Visit my website at CassidyDiehl.com to sign up!

ABOUT THE AUTHOR

A visionary bridge builder between the humankind and the cosmos, Cassidy Diehl helps people connect to the unity consciousness of their own spirit through a series of holistic methods she uses to materialize the divine fabric of universal oneness. She deprograms the 3rd dimensional energy of duality to help people heal many lifetimes of experiences of divisiveness and separation, so they can come out of those old identifications and smallness of it. Her passion is serving humanity to reach greater freedom from hierarchy and separation in their worth, while feeling energetically expansive and united with themselves as universal beings of light.

Visit her website www.CassidyDiehl.com

Made in the USA
Middletown, DE
15 November 2018